Be a Pink Dolphin

In a world where you can be anything...

Marya Patrice Sherron

KI PRODUCTIONS

Where every story matters

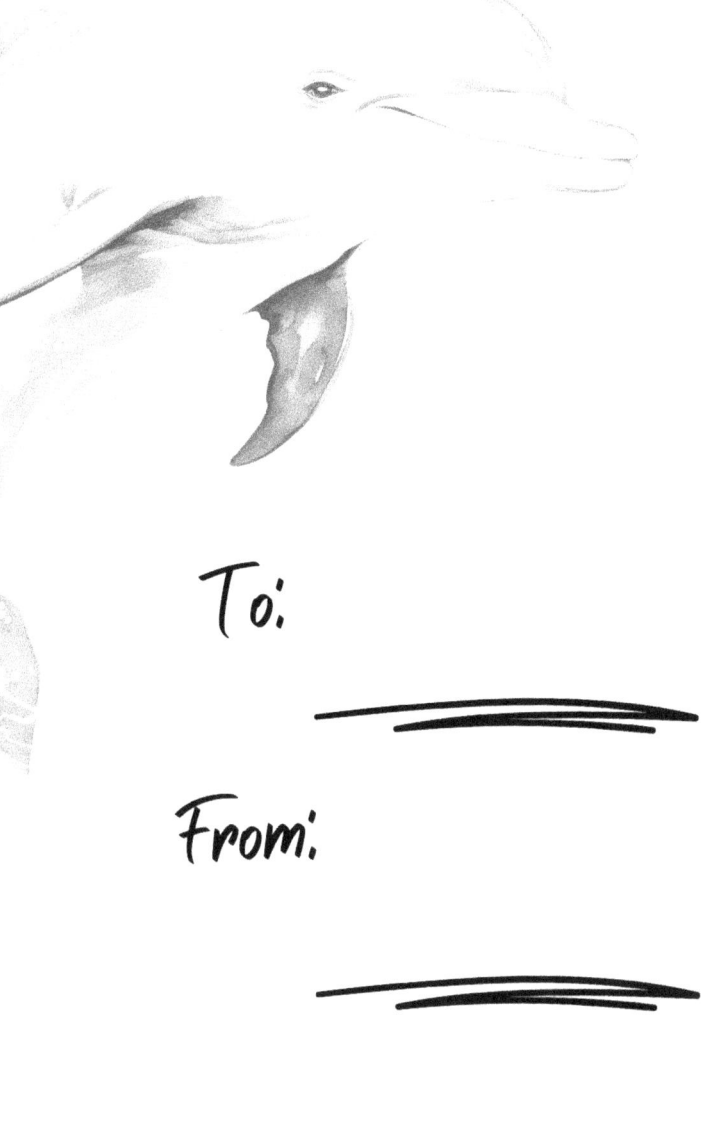

To:

From:

Hello Pink Dolphin,

Less than 1% of the world's dolphin population is pink... that's more rare than a diamond.

I designed this journal for all the Pink Dolphins out there who sometimes feel like they don't fit in or would rather be "normal" (whatever that is?!), or sometimes don't know what to do with all their beautiful uniqueness... this is for you.

May you be Big, Bold, & Pink.
May you fall in love with everything that makes you different.
May you make an unapologetic splash everywhere you go.
May You See Yourself in all of Your Splendor.
May you show other Pink Dolphins the way.

xoxo
Marya

Fun Facts About
Pink Dolphins

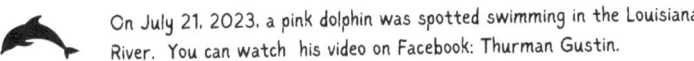 On July 21, 2023, a pink dolphin was spotted swimming in the Louisiana River. You can watch his video on Facebook: Thurman Gustin.

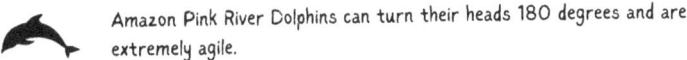 Amazon Pink River Dolphins can turn their heads 180 degrees and are extremely agile.

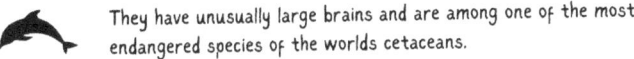 They have unusually large brains and are among one of the most endangered species of the worlds cetaceans.

 Amazon Pink River Dolphins can blush.

"BE YOURSELF.
EVERYONE ELSE IS
TAKEN."
— OSCAR WILDE

_____

_____

_____

_____

_____

_____

_____

_____

_____

_____

_____

_____

_____

_____

_____

_____

_____

_____

_____

_____

"To be yourself in a world that is constantly trying to make you something else is the greatest accomplishment."
—Ralph Waldo Emerson

_____

_____

_____

_____

_____

_____

_____

_____

_____

_____

_____

"THE THINGS THAT MAKE ME DIFFERENT ARE THE THINGS THAT MAKE ME."
– WINNIE THE POOH

_____

_____

_____

_____

_____

_____

_____

_____

_____

_____

_____

_____

_____

_____

_____

_____

_____

_____

_____

_____

_____

_____

_____

_____

_____

_____

_____

_____

_____

_____

_____

_____

_____

"You are unique. You have different talents and abilities. You don't have to always follow in the footsteps of others. And most importantly, you should always remind yourself that you don't have to do what everyone else is doing and have a responsibility to develop the talents you have been given."
— Roy T. Bennett

_____

_____

_____

_____

_____

_____

_____

_____

_____

_____

_____

_____

_____

_____

_____

_____

_____

_____

_____

_____

_____

_____

THE ONE WHO FOLLOWS THE CROWD WILL USUALLY GO NO FURTHER THAN THE CROWD. THOSE WHO WALK ALONE ARE LIKELY TO FIND THEMSELVES IN PLACES NO ONE HAS EVER SEEN BEFORE."
-ALBERT EINSTEIN

_____

_____

_____

_____

_____

_____

_____

_____

_____

_____

"IN ORDER TO BE IRREPLACEABLE, ONE MUST ALWAYS BE DIFFERENT."
— COCO CHANEL

_____

_____

_____

_____

_____

_____

_____

_____

_____

_____

_____

"Normal is not something to aspire to. It's something to get away from."
– Jodie Foster

"I thought not fitting in was something I had to fix. Now I see it as my superpower."
— Maxime Lagacé

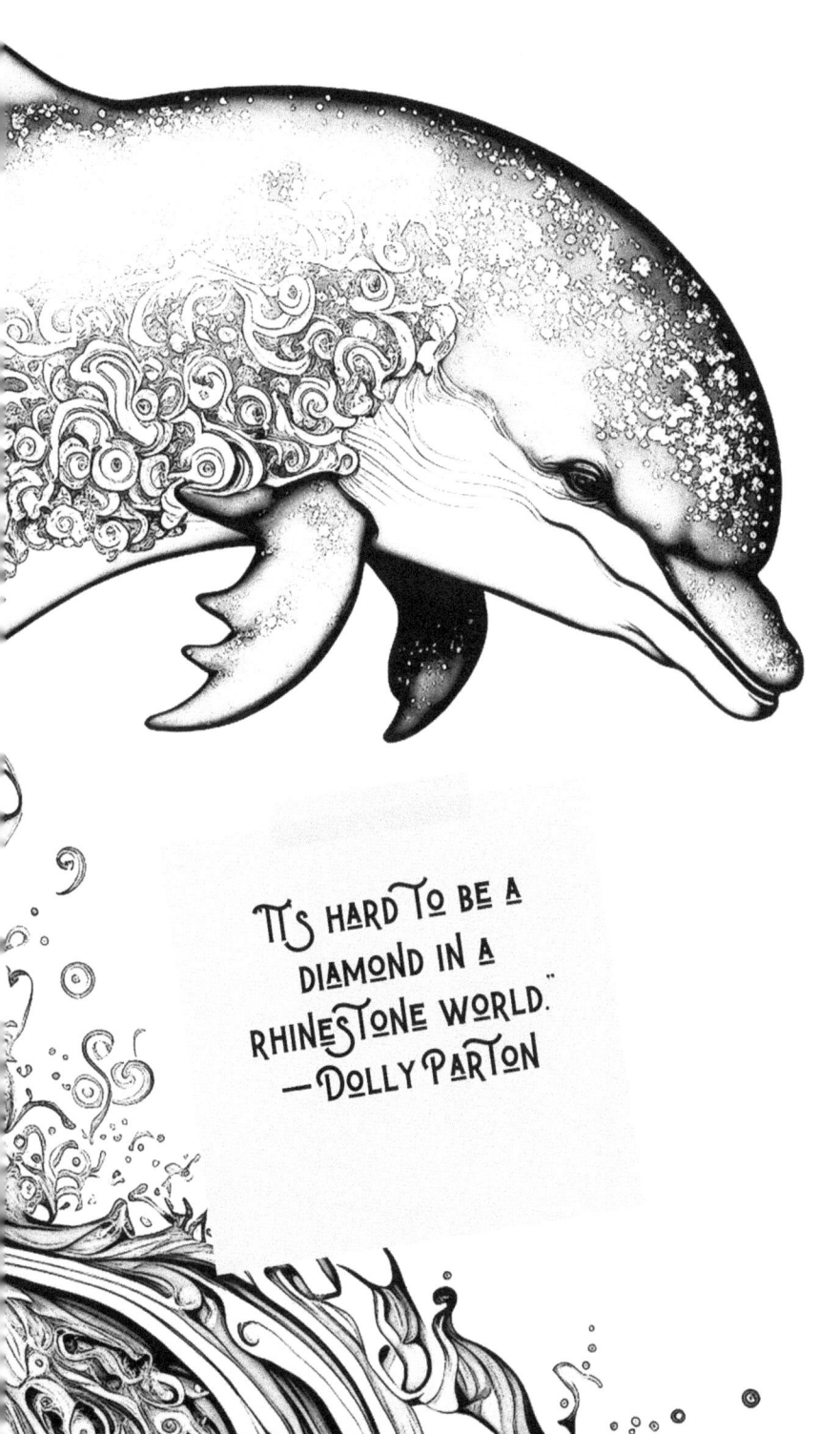

"It's hard to be a diamond in a rhinestone world."
—Dolly Parton

_____

_____

_____

_____

_____

_____

_____

_____

_____

_____

_____

_____

_____

_____

_____

_____

_____

_____

_____

_____

"IMPOSSIBLE IS JUST AN OPINION."
—PAULO COELHO

_____

_____

_____

_____

_____

_____

_____

_____

_____

_____

_____

"IF YOU'RE A PINK DOLPHIN.
GO AHEAD AND BLUSH... YOU
ARE THE RAREST OF RARE
AND UTTERLY MAGICAL."
-MARYA PATRICE SHERRON

_____

_____

_____

_____

_____

_____

_____

_____

_____

_____

_____

_____

_____

_____

_____

_____

_____

_____

_____

_____

_____

You're
magnificent

"You may not control all the events that happen to you. But you can decide not to be reduced by them."
— Maya Angelou

"Never dull your shine for
somebody else."
— Tyra Banks